DANNY TEMPLAR

THE PYRAMID PUZZLE

Written by
Alec Sillifant

Illustrated by
Barrie Appleby

mea
CHIL

D0626457

CHAPTER 1

Spending the first day of his school summer holidays stuck in his bedroom playing 'Treasure of Atlantis' on his video console was not the best thing he could think of doing. But as he had just moved into a new house in a new area, and he didn't know anyone, Danny didn't have much choice in the matter.

With his mum and dad both working and his Aunty Mabel, who was looking after him, practising 'Extreme Knitting' or her 'my haven't you grown' lines. Danny was left to his own amusement. His own amusement, at this time, being to play the video game he'd completed twice already.

'Jump over the pit; swing on the rope; arm wrestle the gorilla...' thought Danny with boredom, as he negotiated the familiar catacombs of the sunken city...again.

'Round the spinning swords; jump the poison darts...hold on, something different,' thought Danny.

'I've never noticed that before.'

Danny expertly guided the muscle-bound archaeologist over to a crack in the rock walls and, with a press of the 'X' button, he made him pull a lever.

A hidden door slid aside to reveal a cavern where a cage was hanging above a boiling pit of lava. The cage was held up by a rope that was being gradually sliced through by a spinning blade.

Inside this doomed cage was a figure, pacing up and down, that stopped every other pace to shake at the bars that kept him captive.

Then something very weird happened; Danny thought the figure in the iron cage looked straight at him and said, "Jolly good, old man. A bit of help, what?"

Danny smiled as he studied the new character. He was dressed like he was ready to go on safari in khaki shorts, khaki shirt and a pith helmet.

"What a weird looking character," he said, thinking aloud.

"I say, old chap," said the figure in the cage. "There's no need to be rude. Don't you think I'm suffering enough?"

Danny's smile faded. "You can hear me?"

"Of course I can hear you," replied the figure. "Now are you going to get me out of here or what? What."

"Er..." said Danny, a little confused by the advanced game play he'd uncovered. "I'll try." He looked around the cavern because, as any gamer knows, there is always a way out of every sticky situation.

He soon spotted a silver keypad embedded in the rock wall. "I think this may have something to do with your problem," said Danny.

"Splendid," said the trapped victim, as the cage suddenly jerked and dropped nearer the lava. "Though I think speed may be of the essence, old bean, don't you?"

Danny moved the muscle-bound archaeologist to the keypad and read aloud the notice that hung above it.

"THE MORE YOU HAVE OF IT, THE LESS YOU SEE."

"Curse Dr Weevilpoop," spat the caged figure.

"Who?" said Danny.

"Dr Weevilpoop," repeated the prisoner. "He's the evil genius who put me in this cage and he has this thing for riddles."

"I see," said Danny, who was really very impressed with the level of interactive game play that he had stumbled upon.

The cage jerked down again as the blade sliced further through the rope.

"Could you hurry up, old bean," said the figure in the cage, looking quite worried. "Things are beginning to look a little dark."

"That's it," shouted Danny. "The more you have of it, the less you see. Darkness, darkness is the answer."

"Jolly good show," shouted the captive. "I'd have got that too, you know, but my arms were too far away from the pad. Type it in then and let's see what happens."

Danny tapped away at his control pad.

'D...A...R...K...N...E...S...S'

A side of the cage sprang
open just as the rope holding it was
severed. It plunged into the red-hot
lava with an eruption of orange
sparks and flames.

'Oh well,' thought Danny as he reached over for the reset button. 'I'll just have to restart the game and do it again.'

"Splendid job, that man," cried a voice and the newly freed captive's face filled the screen.

Danny was a little shocked.

"H…how did you get out of that?"

"Rocket boots, old chap," smiled the face. "Standard issue you know. Jolly useful in a tight spot."

"I suppose they are," agreed Danny. "And now I suppose you are going to give me the next clue so I can open other secret levels in the game?"

"Game?" said the frowning face. "What game, old boy? Not unless you consider the whole world being in danger a game."

"Well I…" started Danny before this mysterious new character in 'Treasures of Atlantis' spoke again.

"Of course you don't, and I can tell an agent like you could be very handy in my current mission."

Danny stared wide-eyed at the screen. This was computer gaming at an amazing level. He'd never seen anything like this before.

"Anyway old chap," said the figure. "Must fly, I'll be in touch." With that he was gone, his boots blasting him away leaving nothing more than a trail of sparks behind him before the screen went black.

"That was way too cool," muttered Danny, hitting the power button and dropping his control pad on the floor. "I'll have to save up to buy 'Treasure of Atlantis 2' now."

But before he could think any more on the subject the doorbell rang...

CHAPTER 2

Danny opened the door.

"Templar?" said the figure on the doorstep. "Danny Templar?"

Danny looked in amazement as he recognised the safari suit and pith helmet. "You're..."

14

"Baron Fortseque-Smythe," said the big man in khaki, twisting the monocle he wore. "But Baron will do fine, old chap."

"But…you were just in my video game," stuttered Danny, rather unsure what was going on.

"And a damned fine job you did there Templar," smiled the Baron. "Thought I was a goner for sure that time, what?"

Danny tried to speak several times, but he didn't know what to say or where to start.

The Baron looked at his wrist watch. "Look old chap, I'd love to stand here and watch you pull silly faces all day but as I've said before I'm on rather an important mission to save the world and time is of the essence, so Templar, are you in or not?"

Suddenly there was a sound like a cat playing the violin with its tongue.

"What on earth is that noise, old chap?" said the Baron, trying to look round Danny.

"It's my Aunty Mabel doing Tai Chi on the telly," said Danny with a weak smile.

"Really, what channel is she on?" asked the Baron.

There was a high pitched scream followed by a lot of crashing sound.

"It's not a TV programme," said Danny, wincing at the sound of destruction. "She does it on the telly."

"Oh," said the Baron. "It sounds like her balance needs a little work." Danny nodded, thinking to himself, 'Mental balance mostly'.

The Baron looked at his watch again and hissed. "Sorry about rushing you, old bean, but I need to know now if I can use your brain or not?"

"My brain!" gasped Danny.

"While it's still in your head of course," smiled the Baron. "I'm one of the good guys. One doesn't do things like that, what. After seeing you act cool as you like to get me out of that cage, I knew you'd be the perfect assistant for this mission."

"But how come you know my name, where I live…?" began Danny, but the Baron cut him short.

"Plenty of time for all that later, Templar," said the Baron tapping his watch. "Are you in or out, old chap?"

Danny looked at the Baron, then back into the house from where he could hear his Aunty Mabel chanting.

'Not much of a choice,' he thought. 'Stay here and spend my time hiding from Aunty Mabel in my room or...' Danny didn't know what the 'or' was but it had to be better, didn't it?

"Okay," said Danny, nodding his head. "I'm in."

"Jolly good, old chap," beamed the Baron. "To the Morpho-Jet we go."

"The what-o jet?" asked Danny.

"The Morpho-Jet," repeated the Baron. "Damned fine piece of equipment that conceals itself by fitting in with the surroundings. Tell you what, old bean, see if you can find it."

Without hesitation Danny pointed and said, "Would it be the twenty foot high marble water feature in the front garden that wasn't there ten minutes ago?"

"Okay," said the Baron sulkily. "It has one or two glitches but it's still jolly clever, what?"

Danny had to agree it was jolly clever and even more so when the Baron pressed a button on a key fob in his hand and the huge 'water feature' changed into what looked like a giant chrome spearhead.

"Wow!" gasped Danny excitedly.

"Wow, indeed," smiled the Baron. "I can see you're impressed with that, aren't you Templar?"

Danny ran his hand down the smooth side of the Morpho-Jet. "How fast does it go?"

The Baron pressed another button on the fob and a hatch slid open to reveal two seats side by side in front of a control panel.

"I don't think fast is a quick enough word to describe her," said the Baron. "Put it this way, old bean, that cave you just rescued me from was in Indonesia."

Danny looked amazed.

"But that was only quarter of an hour ago…at most."

"Exactly," beamed the Baron. "She's that fast. Come on, climb aboard Templar. Time flies and all that, what?"

Danny followed the Baron and took the seat next to the strange new acquaintance he'd made. In front of them was an array of lights and screens, the like of which Danny had only ever seen in science fiction films. "This is amazing."

"'Tis rather," agreed the Baron, as the hatch silently closed about them. "Rather expensive too, so I would appreciate it if you didn't touch anything."

Danny sat quietly as the Baron flicked switches and studied the screens about him. "Anything I can help with before we take off, Baron?"

The Baron smiled. "We have taken off. In fact, your Aunty Mabel is probably doing her Tai Chi over two hundred miles behind us by now. We've just flown over the Eiffel Tower in France. I told you she was fast, old chap."

"Smooth too," Danny whispered to himself.

"Tell you what, Templar," said the Baron pointing to a screen. "You can keep an eye on this for me."

Danny looked up at the display. "What are the green dots on it?"

"Other air traffic," said the Baron flicking a switch. "Holiday flights, military aircraft that kind of thing. The Morpho-Jet avoids obstacles automatically. The screen is just there for back up, old chap. It's when we get red dots things get really fun," said the Baron laughing.

"I see," said Danny rubbing his chin. "And the red ones would be...?"

"Well, that would mean Dr Weevilpoop has sent some of his robotic minions on a 'seek and destroy' mission."

"I see," said Danny, slowly.

"So if I were to say there are three red dots that appear to be approaching very quickly on the screen it would not be good?"

"Rather, Templar," smiled the Baron. "In fact I would probably say something like 'jolly bad show' and start sweating."

"There are three red dots that appear to be approaching very quickly," said Danny.

The Baron took a quick look at the screen then sat back in his seat. "Jolly bad show," he said and began to sweat.

CHAPTER 3

"Can't we just blast them out of the sky?" asked Danny.

"I think you need to know that the Mark Two Morpho-Jet is fitted with the latest in hi-tech weaponry, old boy," said the Baron. "Heat-seeking missiles, laser cannons and various remotely operated magnetic mines."

"Well," said Danny. "What are you waiting for?"

"Sadly, this model is a Mark One," shrugged the Baron.

"So we've got no weapons?" shrieked Danny, as something exploded close to the Morpho-Jet.

"I think there may be a pea-shooter in the glove box," answered the Baron with a smirk.

"This is not the time for jokes," said Danny. "Especially bad ones! There must be something we can do. Can't we evade them or outrun them or something?"

"We're on auto-pilot, old chap," explained the Baron. "The Morpho-Jet plots the quickest and safest course and sticks to it until it gets there, what?"

Another explosion rocked the aircraft.

"Surely there's got to be a manual override. At least then we can try to dodge their shots."

"There is, old chap," said the Baron.

The Baron flicked a button and a control pad emerged from the control console. A message on the main screen read,

'AUTO-PILOT DISENGAGED'.

There was a long pause while the perplexed Baron stared at the control pad. Finally, Danny said "Well?"

"Slight problem, old chap."

"You can't fly it, can you?" guessed Danny.

"Of course I can," snapped the Baron. "I'm just a bit rusty, old chap."

"Really," said Danny, grabbing the control pad as another explosion rattled even closer to the Morpho-Jet. "Well, in my experience, it's always just a matter of figuring out what control does what. Right, I think we'll start with this button…"

Danny and the Baron were pushed back into their seats as the Morpho-Jet began to hurtle toward the ground.

"I think it would be a jolly good idea if you could find the 'up' button next," suggested the Baron, finding it hard to speak as his face was squashed and twisted by the G-force.

Danny quickly pressed another button and the Morpho-Jet span upside down.

"Are those robot things still on our tail?"

The Baron checked the screen.

"Yes, old bean, but I think they have stopped shooting at us and are going to wait for us to smash ourselves up instead."

"Give me a chance," said Danny, frantically pressing buttons as the Morpho-Jet tumbled, twisted and swung side to side like a sock in a washing machine. "I'm just getting the hang of it."

"Hope so, old chap," said the Baron. "Because I think the kippers one had for breakfast will be awfully hard to clean up."

Suddenly the Morpho-Jet levelled out and began to fly smoothly again. "Got it," grinned Danny, his fingers tapping expertly over the buttons. "Just like flying the starship in 'Martian Invasion 3'. Right, let's give these robot things a taste of their own medicine."

The Baron frowned. "No weapons, remember, my good man."

"There's more than one way to crack an egg, Baron," said Danny, with a grin.

"Really," said the Baron. "How many, old chap?"

Danny shook his head as he continued to fly the Morpho-Jet. "Just watch the screen and let me know when the robots have got us surrounded."

"Okay-dokey, Templar," nodded the Baron.

Danny flew the Morpho-Jet like an expert, tapping at the buttons to make it dive, climb and swoop in every direction, from upside down to downside up, but smoothly enough to keep the Baron's breakfast in place.

"Steady..." said the Baron, with his eyes fixed to the screen.

"Steady...NOW!"

Danny jammed his thumb onto a red button and, immediately, the Morpho-Jet slammed to a dead stop.

Above their heads, Danny and the Baron could hear the hiss of passing missiles, then loud explosions and then, with a final thunderous boom, the three red dots disappeared from the screen.

"Jolly good show, Templar"

shouted the Baron. "I knew you were the man for the job all along and passing my test like that just proved it."

"Test? What test?"

"My test to see if you could handle such things under pressure, old bean," said the Baron.

"In actual fact, I would have done exactly the same manoeuvres myself, only a little more expertly."

"I see," said Danny, not believing a word.

"So are you going to fly us the rest of the way on manual then?"

The Baron shook his head.

"Rather thought you could work on smoothing out some of your skills, what? I'll do the navigating." Before Danny could argue, the Baron added, "Due south-east, old boy, and we'll be there in no time."

In no time, Danny was landing the Morpho-Jet without the slightest of bumps and the canopy was sliding open.

"I can't believe we're in Egypt," said Danny, looking all around.

The Baron jumped down from the cockpit onto the ground.

"Sand, camels and pyramids," he said. "I think you can believe we're in Egypt, unless Blackpool has changed a lot since I was last there, old chap."

Danny sneered at the sarcastic comment but thought better of saying anything. He did quite fancy going home after all this was over and it would be a very long walk without the Morpho-Jet.

"Templar, old boy," shouted the Baron. "Grab the rucksack from behind the seats, there's a good chap."

Danny found the rucksack, picked it up and jumped down from the Morpho-Jet. "There you go."

He handed it to the Baron who looked puzzled.

"What are you doing, old chap?"

"You told me you wanted your rucksack," answered Danny.

"Indeed old chap," smiled the Baron. "And I want you to carry it. Now chop-chop, we haven't got much time. I reckon Dr Weevilpoop can't be far behind...at least I hope he's behind!"

As Danny ground his teeth and struggled to slip the rucksack over his shoulders, the Baron pressed his key fob and the Morpho-Jet morphed to blend into its new surroundings.

The two passengers looked in silence at the Morpho-Jet's new disguise for a few moments.

"That's just asking for attention out here," noted Danny.

"Probably, old chap," agreed the Baron. "Still, not much we can do about it now," he added cheerfully.

"Right now, we need to be at the smallest of those three pyramids over there. Best foot forward, what?" And with that the Baron strode out, closely followed by Danny, who couldn't help looking back at the Morpho-Jet every so often and shaking his head.

CHAPTER 4

Danny followed his new comrade, who was carefully studying the stones of the pyramid. "What exactly are we looking for?" he asked.

"The way in of course, old chap," replied the Baron without looking up from the wall of the pyramid.

"I assumed that much," sighed Danny. "I mean what are we looking for once we get in?"

"Cleopatra's Eye, old bean," said the Baron, as he continued his search amongst the stones.

Danny winced. "Won't it be a little dried out and rotten by now?"

The Baron smiled. "Not the old girl's actual eye, old man. It's a diamond."

"Just a diamond?" said Danny, very unimpressed.

"It's far from being 'just a diamond', Templar old chap. Cleopatra's Eye is the purest gem the world has ever seen and if used in laser technology would produce a weapon of devastating power."

"And I suppose somebody is trying to do that, are they?"

"Indeed," said the Baron running his hand across a huge square slab.

"Dr Weevilpoop and his minions have already got a satellite orbiting the earth. Our intelligence indicates it's ready to have Cleopatra's Eye installed and then he'll be able to hold the whole world to ransom."

Danny nodded his head. "But weren't the treasures of the pyramids taken years ago by tomb raiders."

The Baron leapt up and looked about madly. "Tomb raider? Where? Where is she?"

Danny sighed. "I said 'tomb raiders'...thieves...that kind of thing."

The Baron calmed down again. "Oh right, I see. I thought you meant... it's just that Croft woman has been a real thorn in our side for years, old bean – a real thorn." He continued his search.

"What it is Templar, old chap, the ancient Egyptians were rather clever when it came to keeping the real treasures hidden. Oh yes, they left a lot of dubious stuff around to satisfy the thieves but the really valuable stuff they hid much more cunningly." The Baron stopped and smiled.

"Like here for example."

Danny looked at the small carving that the Baron was pointing to on the stone. "It doesn't look much like a way in to me."

"Exactly, old chap," said the Baron.

"Would you be so kind and pass me the rucksack, there's a good chap."

Danny passed the rucksack and the Baron lifted up the flap to reveal a keypad.

"What's that?"

"This," said the Baron, "is an agent's best friend. I'd be lost without this, old bean. Just type in whichever piece of equipment you need from headquarters and it's beamed into the rucksack."

The Baron tapped away on the pad and then put his hand into the bag to pull out a smelly, wet haddock.

"Don't tell me," said Danny. "It's got a few glitches."

The Baron tried again and this time retrieved what looked like a pocket calculator. "Jolly good, the ancient languages translator." He switched it on and aimed it at the carving on the rock. "In a couple of seconds the translator will crack the code of the hieroglyphs and we'll be in...No time at all...any second now...you and me on the way to get Cleopatra's Eye, old chap...Nothing to stop us at all..."

"It can't translate it, can it?" said Danny.

"No," the Baron sighed throwing the unit back into the rucksack. "Still, chin up, old chap. We can work it out for ourselves, what. Now let's take a look. There's a chap standing under what looks like the sun waving his arms in the air. What do you reckon, young Templar?"

"Well..." began Danny.

"Got it, old chap," shouted the Baron. "If I have understood this right, we need to dance like a chicken under the baking Egyptian sun."

"Well, that's one explanation..." Danny began.

But the Baron was off, flapping his bent arms like wings, clucking and bobbing his head as if picking corn off the ground. "Come on Templar, join in, old bean," he said between 'clucks'. "Do you want to save the world or what, what?"

Danny smiled weakly at the Baron as he danced like a madman under the blazing desert sun, then he turned his attention to look more closely at the carving again. There was indeed a figure standing under the sun with his arms out but there appeared to be something else below it, covered by sand. Danny brushed away the sand

that was hiding the rest of the clue. It was a long black line that came to rest on a small carving of a pyramid.

"I wonder," muttered Danny, standing up until his back was directly facing the sun.

Slowly he raised his arms and watched as the shadow of his hands came to rest on the stone with the carvings on.

It was strange; although only his shadow was touching the rock, he could feel it against his own fingers. Danny took a step forward and the rock moved. He took another and the rock moved again. Danny Templar was moving the rock with his shadow alone.

With his third step the rock moved even further in, then slid to the side with a thundering thud.

The Baron stopped his mad chicken dance as he heard the noise.

"Whizzo," he cried in triumph. "Who'd have thought that dancing like a chicken could be so powerful, what? Still, I was poultry in motion, hey Templar?"

Danny lowered his arms and grinned at the bad joke. "What next?"

"We go in, old chap," said the Baron, excitedly tapping the keypad on the rucksack and pulling out torches and a map of the London Underground, at which he frowned. "Luckily I memorised the maze of tunnels before I left HQ, what."

"Is it dangerous?" asked Danny.

"Not really," replied the Baron

quickly stepping through the pyramid wall. "Just stick close to me and we'll be fine."

Danny shrugged and stepped in.

"Right let me think," said the Baron, shining his torch into the pitch black of the tunnel. "Ah, yes, I remember. East for the first fifty paces and then…"

Danny and the Baron plummeted downward as the floor of the tunnel dropped them into a huge chute.

"Been on your holidays yet, Templar?" asked the Baron, when they had stopped screaming.

"No," answered Danny shining his torch onto his watch. "Aren't you concerned we've been sliding down this chute for over ten minutes?"

"Really," said the Baron. "That long? Told you they hid the real treasures well, didn't I, Templar? In that case in any second we should come to land on the shore of an underground lake..."

Danny and the Baron landed with two dusty thuds as the chute came to an abrupt end.

The Baron stood up and dusted off his safari suit. "Ah, here we are, old chap, an underground lake filled with..."

CHAPTER 5

"Crocodiles!" shouted Danny,
as he stared at hundreds of green,
snapping jaws.

"Well done, Templar," said the Baron cleaning his monocle. "A lot of people might have thought those blighters were alligators. Actually, these are White Nile crocodiles, a particularly vicious breed with the Latin name Greenus Biteyabum."

Danny, keeping his eyes on the rather hungry looking reptiles, said, "Aren't you worried by this?"

The Baron replaced his monocle and smiled. "Of course not, old chap. I saw this in a movie once. All we have to do is wait for the crocs to line up in just the right way then run across the tops of their heads to the other side of the lake."

"Don't you think that's a little bit too..."

"Tally Ho!" shouted the Baron as he sprinted toward the crocodiles.

"...mad," finished Danny.

After several minutes of a frantic and deadly game of hopscotch, the Baron threw himself to the safety of the far shore, his safari suit hanging off him like rags.

"You okay?" asked Danny.

"Never better," smiled the Baron, pushing one of his shirt buttons. Instantly, his safari suit began to repair itself and his boots pushed out the odd crocodile tooth. "I say old chap, how did you...?"

"A bridge," said Danny, pointing to the wooden structure that safely spanned the lake. "I figured the Ancient Egyptians would rather keep

both their legs and so I looked round and found a hidden lever which lowered the bridge from the ceiling."

"Well done, Templar," said the Baron. "You keep passing my tests with flying colours, old boy. I'll make a decent operative out of you yet."

"But..." began Danny.

"Right then, Templar," interrupted the Baron. "Once more onto the beach, as they say, what?"

"Is there much further to go before we find Cleopatra's Eye?" asked Danny, as he followed the Baron toward a wall that contained the entrances to three tunnels.

"Not too far, old chap," said the Baron, looking at each tunnel in turn, rubbing his chin and wearing a puzzled frown.

"Okay," said Danny. "Let me put it another way. Are there any more lakes full of crocodiles?"

"Don't be silly," laughed the Baron. "Do you know how hard it is to construct such a feature, old chap? Even for the clever old Egyptians. No, from now on in it's plain sailing all the way...unless you pick the wrong corridor then it's snake pits, poison darts and collapsing roofs."

Danny was starting to get a suspicious feeling in his stomach. "You do know the right way to go, don't you?"

"Of course, old chap," said the Baron. "I told you I memorised the map before I left HQ."

For a little while Danny and the Baron looked at the three tunnels in silence. Then the Baron said, "Eeny-Meany-Miney-Mo. This way Templar," and he strode into the tunnel on the left.

Danny shook his head and followed. Several minutes past before they re-emerged followed by a cloud of dust.

"Your training is going rather well, Templar. Did you see the way I let you rescue me from getting crushed by those falling rocks? Jolly well done, old chap."

Danny just about managed a smile. "You're welcome, Baron."

"Right," said the Baron looking at the two remaining tunnels. "I'd best pick this time, old bean. We don't want another near disaster on our hands, what?"

"But I didn't..." protested Danny.

"Don't blame yourself, Templar. You're new to this; it's only to be expected," interrupted the Baron before adding, "Of course, it's obviously this one. Don't know how you missed it." The Baron bounded into the middle tunnel.

Seconds later the Baron came sprinting back out of the tunnel, eyes wide with fear, and a terrible wild roaring echoing from the tunnel behind him. "I suddenly remember," said the Baron, grabbing Danny by the arm and forcing him to run. "It's the one on the right."

In a few minutes, the Baron and Danny were shining their torches on a black door of immense size, the like of which neither of them had seen before.

"Have you ever seen the like of such a black door of immense size before, Templar, old chap?" said the Baron.

"No," said Danny smirking.

"What's so funny, Templar?" asked the Baron.

"You look like you've just sat on a hedgehog," replied Danny, shining his torch onto the seat of the Baron's shorts.

The Baron looked at the spikes.

"I say, I do rather," he said smiling. "It's a good job I put on my poison dart proof underpants this morning. Don't you think?"

"If you'd followed the pattern on

the floor like I'd said, you wouldn't have triggered the trap," noted Danny.

"I knew that," argued the Baron. "It was all part of your..."

"Training," finished Danny with a smile.

"Quite, old chap," said the Baron. "Now shall we open the door and collect old Cleopatra's Eye?"

"Why not," said Danny, and they pushed against the black door of immense size. To their surprise it opened, as easily as a black door not of immense size, to reveal a room cloaked in darkness.

"What we need here..." said the Baron tapping at the rucksack's keypad. "...is some light." He pulled out a pair of jeans with extremely wide legs. The Baron frowned and tapped again. "Ah, that's better," he said holding up a different type of flares.

"Now all I need to find is the...ah, and here it is."

The Baron pulled the cords on the flares, which burst into life and dropped them into a golden dish.

In an instant the room was bathed in light.

"Wow," said Danny.

"That's amazing!"

"Clever, what?" smiled the Baron. "Incredible what the Egyptians could do with a golden dish and several hundred mirrors."

With light being reflected into every corner of the room Danny and the Baron could see they were in a richly adorned cavern. Gold and jewels lay around in untidy piles on the floor; hieroglyphics had been carved neatly into every space on the walls and fine silks hung from the ceiling. It must have been the biggest treasure trove the world had ever seen. And right in the middle, on its own stone column, surrounded by ten-foot high marble statues of Egyptian warriors armed to the teeth, was a magnificent diamond.

"I do believe we have found what we were looking for, Templar, old bean," smiled the Baron, bounding over to the diamond.

Danny was starting to get a funny feeling. "Don't you think this is a bit too easy?"

"Nonsense, old chap," smiled the Baron, bending down to pick up a ruby of similar size to Cleopatra's Eye. "I saw it in a movie once."

"I saw that movie too," said Danny. "And a huge great boulder came crashing down from the roof."

The Baron had a quick look above his head.

"No boulders here, Templar. Everything is tickety-boo." And with that he snatched up the diamond and dropped the ruby in its place. "See, piece of cake, what."

After a few moments Danny began to relax and was just about to say 'Maybe you're right' when the sound of a black door of immense size, closing itself, stopped him. He turned to the Baron, who wasn't looking at the door at all but, instead, had a strange look of surprise on his face.

"Well I must admit," said the Baron slowly. "This didn't happen in the movie I saw..."

CHAPTER 6

"I told you it was too easy," shouted Danny, ducking to avoid the blade of a rather rusty old sword.

The Baron opened his mouth to answer but Danny beat him to it. "And don't say it's all part of my training." Danny leapt to the side as a spear thudded into the wall behind him. "We need to get out of here, Baron, and the only way I can see is the way we came in."

Danny and the Baron dodged around the marble warriors, avoiding deadly weapon strikes, until they both stood breathing heavily by the door. They pushed with all their strength but it stayed firmly closed.

"What about the rucksack?" said Danny, keeping an eye on the advancing warriors. "Anything in there that can help us?"

"Possibly," said the Baron. "I believe I left it on the floor by this door."

"Where?" said Danny, looking around frantically. "I can't see it."

"You won't old chap, it's on the floor on the other side of the door," explained the Baron, with a weak apologetic smile.

Danny's shoulders dropped and he looked again at the warriors behind them. "I don't suppose it would be worth running."

"Probably not, old chap," agreed the Baron. "With no way out they'd catch us eventually."

The warrior's heavy footsteps brought them nearer and nearer and, with each step, they raised their vicious weapons a little higher.

The Baron gave a little cough, straightened his shoulders and put out his hand to Danny. "It's been a real honour working with you Templar, old chap. Without you, I wouldn't have got anywhere near this far, what?"

Danny couldn't help but smile as he shook the Baron's hand. "Anytime, Baron, it's been fun...right up until this bit anyway."

"Toodle pip, Templar."

"Yeah, see you around Baron."

The marble warriors stopped and readied their weapons to make one final devastating attack and then one of them exploded into a cloud of dust. The remaining animated statues turned round and, as they did so, a second was destroyed.

Danny and the Baron didn't let this opportunity pass them by. They sprinted from the door and dived for cover behind a large golden throne.

"What's going on?" said Danny.

"I'm not really that sure, old chap" said the Baron. "But, judging by the exploding rock soldiers and high pitched 'zinging', I would say someone is firing heavy laser weapons."

Soon the sound of explosions and firing laser weapons stopped and, from this new stillness in the room, there came a mocking voice. "Come out, come out, wherever you are?"

"Who's that?" whispered Danny.

The Baron carefully sneaked his head round the throne and then quickly drew it back.

"Curses," he muttered. "It's Dr Weevilpoop and he's got quite a few of his android solders with him."

"Come on," shouted Dr Weevilpoop. "I haven't got all day, there's a world that needs enslaving and I know you're behind the throne."

Danny and the Baron looked at each other, shrugged their shoulders and stood up. Before them, on top of an earth tunnelling machine stood a tall man dressed in black and wearing a red cape. Several matt black robots carrying laser rifles accompanied him.

"We meet at last, Fortseque-Smythe," Weevilpoop sneered.

"Actually we've met before," corrected the Baron. "It's hard for a chap to forget a cad like you."

The evil doctor sighed. "I know that, and you know that, but it's all part of being the bad guy. We have certain lines we must use, you've got your catchphrases and I've got mine, okay? In fact here's another one... hand over the diamond."

"Diamond, old chap?" said the Baron scratching his head. "Do you know what he's on about Templar?"

Danny shook his head.

Dr Weevilpoop grinned evilly.

"I'm so glad you said that, now I can vaporize you and take it from the piles of ashes that were your puny bodies. Blast them!"

Danny and the Baron dived back down behind the throne as laser bolts blasted all around them.

"Any ideas, Templar, old chap?" said the Baron.

"Actually," whispered Danny. "I think the ancient Egyptians solved this one for us. Help me drag that golden shield over."

"Oh I get it, old chap, splendid idea," agreed the Baron as he and Danny pulled the valuable shield toward them. "Ready?"

Danny nodded and they stood up holding the shield before them. All of Dr Weevilpoop's robots aimed at the shield and fired their laser rifles. For a few seconds there was 'zinging' and 'pinging' as laser beams hit the shield and instantly reflected back off the polished surface, then once again the room fell silent.

"What!" screamed Weevilpoop. "Not my beautiful robot minions.

The Baron and Danny lowered the shield to see Weevilpoop jumping up and down in rage, his robots destroyed by their own weapons.

"We've still got the problem of Weevilpoop to deal with, old chap," said the Baron.

"Maybe not," said Danny looking round the room. "If this room is like the ones in every video game I've ever played, right about now it should start to..."

A low, loud rumbling started to shake the room and bits of roof and wall began to crash down.

"...self-destruct," finished Danny.

"What the…" whimpered Dr Weevilpoop as he wobbled on top of his earth tunnelling machine and then fell off to land by the smoking remains of his robots.

"After you Templar, old chap," said the Baron.

"Why thank you," said Danny and he and the Baron dived into the tunnelling machine and quickly closed the door.

"Can you drive this thing, Baron?"

"Of course, old chap," replied the Baron. "This is the bad guy's transport and they're never too bright so everything has to be really simple for them to use, see?"

With that the Baron grabbed the only lever on the control panel and pushed it from the 'DOWN' position to the 'UP' position.

"I must get one of these," said the Baron, as the engines fired up.

"Tally ho!"

"At least getting out was easier than getting in," said Danny, as he and the Baron walked up a sand dune toward the Morpho-Jet.

"Yes, jolly decent of Weevilpoop to let us use his transport," agreed the Baron.

"Do you think he'll escape?"

"Without a doubt, old chap," smiled the Baron. "If there's one thing you can guarantee it's that Weevilpoop will show up every time it looks like things are going well."

The Baron and Danny crested the sand dune and looked down to where the Morpho-Jet, still in disguise, had attracted a very long queue of people.

"I thought an ice cream van in the middle of the desert was asking for trouble," said Danny.

"I have to agree old chap," said the Baron.

"But now we've saved the world, I think ice lollies all round would be a splendid way to celebrate."

"There you go then, old chap," said the Baron, as he landed the Morpho-Jet in Danny's front garden. "Back in time for tea."

"Yeah," said Danny, as he climbed out, a little sorry his adventure was over and he was back to his normal life.

85

"Hold on, old chap," said the Baron, reaching into his pocket.

"Thought, if you wouldn't mind, of course, you might look after this for me. Keep it safe, what."

The Baron placed Cleopatra's Eye into Danny's hand. "Couldn't have done it without you Templar, old boy. You and my expert..."

"Training," said Danny with a smile.

"Exactly, old bean. Well must be off," said the Baron. "Toodle pip."

The Morpho-Jet's upper canopy slid shut and within a second was no more than a dot on the horizon. Danny turned around and went into his house.

"Hello dear," cried Aunty Mabel. "Have you been out having all kinds of adventures?"

"Not really," replied Danny.

"Just saving the world from an evil tyrant with a huge laser in space pointed straight at the earth."

"That's nice," said Aunt Mabel. "I had almost reached spiritual enlightenment but I tripped over the aerial just at the crucial moment. What would you like for tea, dear?"

"Nothing thanks, Aunty Mabel, I'm not hungry."

"Probably been stuffing yourself with ice cream no doubt," smiled Danny's aunt.

"Something like that."

EPILOGUE

As soon as it woke him, Danny had a feeling he knew who it was tapping on his window at three o'clock in the morning and opening his curtains only proved him right.

"Sorry to wake you old chap," said the Baron from the open cockpit of the Morpho-Jet, which was hovering outside Danny's bedroom window.

Danny was still half asleep. "The diamond is still safe," he said rubbing his eyes.

"Didn't think otherwise, old chap," said the Baron. "No, the reason I am here is...well, what do you know about Stonehenge, Templar?"

OTHER FANTASTIC FICTION FROM

meadowside
CHILDREN'S BOOKS

Follow the master of menacing through a maze of mischief and mahem.

£3.99 1-84539-098-9

Grown-ups and softies beware - Dennis is on a mission to menace!

£3.99 1-84539-095-4

OTHER FANTASTIC FICTION FROM

meadowside
CHILDREN'S BOOKS

Everyone knows a menace
somewhere -
Now, read about the
greatest menace ever!

£3.99 1-84539-097-0

Dennis is back! Join the
mighty menace
as he creates more crazy
chaos!

£3.99 1-84539-096-2

SALLY MUDGETT
and the BLUE DRAGON

Susan Chandler Illustrated by Emma Parrish

OTHER FANTASTIC FICTION FROM

CHILDREN'S BOOKS

Sally Mudgett and the Blue Dragon

written by **Susan Chandler**

Professor Mudgett and his daughter, Sally, live in a little house in a rubbish dump and dream of better things. When one of the professor's 'secret formulas' goes wrong Sally throws it into the garden and strange things begin to happen. Enter the world of Sally Mudgett and meet the wacky professor, the blue dragon and an evil restaurant owner who likes to be called The Mighty King Poe!

£3.99 1-84539-100-4

James King of England

written by **Jonny Zucker**

The Royal family is stepping down and a competition is underway to find a suitable successor to the throne.

While Royal advisor Sir Cuthbert Snobbish does his best to block the competition entries, James King finds a way through. Now James and his far-from-Regal family are on their way to Buckingham palace and Sir Cuthbert has a Royal fight on his hands.

£3.99 1-84539-101-2

Astro Gran

written and illustrated by **Nick Ward**

There's nothing Gran likes more than an adventure so when Dad invents a space rocket, she is the first to volunteer to try it out.

When Rodney is trapped inside at the last minute, the pair blast off for the cosmic cruise of a lifetime.

£3.99 1-84539-102-0

For Jamie, Brandon, Jake, Alec
– never turn down an adventure in life
A.S.

For Lauren, Ryan, Jessica, Lee, Ben and Louis
B.A.

First published in 2005
by Meadowside Children's Books
185 Fleet Street, London, EC4A 2HS

Text © Alec Sillifant 2005
Illlustrations © Barrie Appleby 2005
The rights of Alec Sillifant and Barrie Appleby to be identified
as the author and illustrator of this work have been asserted
by them in accordance with the Copyright,
Designs and Patents Act, 1988

A CIP catalogue record for this book
is available from the British Library
Printed and bound in England by William Clowes Ltd, Beccles, Suffolk

10 9 8 7 6 5 4 3 2 1